Happy travels.

During a visit to Majorca in 1984, **Peter Clayton** travelled for the first time on the Palma to Soller train, and then onwards to Puerto de Soller by tram. So enraptured was he with the journey that he attempted to purchase a guide to the railway, but was told that no such book existed. Mindful that several hundred equally enthusiastic tourists enjoy the return journey each day throughout the year, Peter decided that a guide-book should exist. This book is the result of that decision...

In 1988, the *Majorca Daily Bulletin* — the island's highly-respected English language newspaper — organised an international journalism competition to celebrate its silver jubilee. For an article based upon the subject of this book, Peter Clayton won the top prize sponsored by the Majorca Ministry of Tourism.

Dedication

This book is dedicated to the townsfolk of Soller — past and present — for their determination, foresight and self-sacrifice which enabled the construction of one of the world's most wonderful railways; and to Carol and Janet, for allowing two grown men to indulge in boyhood fantasies.

Acknowledgements

The author would like to thank the following people and organisations for their kind and invaluable assistance and co-operation in the preparation of this book:
— Iberia International Airlines of Spain for their most efficient service from Manchester to Palma, via Barcelona.
— Sol Hotels, and in particular the management and staff of Hotel Jaime III Sol, Palma.
— Ferrocarril de Soller S.A., and in particular Sr D. Rafael Sierra Arbide.
— The Narrow Gauge Railway Society.

(Front cover) *A Palma-bound train leaving the last tunnel of the route shortly before arriving at Bunola Station.*

THE IRON ROAD
TO SOLLER

A TRAVELLER'S GUIDE TO MAJORCA'S SOLLER RAILWAY

PETER G. CLAYTON

Roger Lascelles, Cartographic and Travel Publisher
47 York Road, Brentford, Middlesex TW8 OQP. Tel: 081-847 0935

Publication Data

Title	The Iron Road To Soller
Typeface	Photoset in Palatino
Photographs	By the Author & Barry Clayton
Maps & Illus.	By David Peacock
Printing	Kelso Graphics, Kelso, Scotland
ISBN	0 903909 98 7
Edition	This First Jan 1992
Publisher	Roger Lascelles
	47 York Road, Brentford (Middx) TW8 0QP
Copyright	Peter G. Clayton 1991

Distribution

Principal retail sales of this book are through the kiosks at the railway stations at Palma and Soller, Majorca.

Specialist retailers of railway and travel publications are invited to write to the publishers for copies at trade terms.

Africa:	South Africa	- Faradawn, Box 17161, Hillbrow 2038
Americas:	Canada	- International Travel Maps and Books, PO Box 2290, Vancouver BC V6B 3W5
	U.S.A.	- Available through major booksellers with good foreign travel sections
Asia:	India	- English Book Store, 17-L Connaught Circus, PO Box 328, New Delhi 110 001
Australasia:	Australia	- Rex Publications, 15 Huntingdon Street, Crows Nest, N.S.W.
Europe:	Belgium	- Brussels - Peuples et Continents
	Germany	- Available through major booksellers with good foreign travel sections
	GB/Ireland	- Available through all booksellers with good foreign travel sections
	Italy	- Libreria dell 'Automobile, Milano
	Netherlands	- Nilsson & Lamm BV, Weesp
	Denmark	- Copenhagen - Arnold Busck, G.E.C. Gad, Boghallen
	Finland	- Oslo - Arne Gimmes/J.G. Tanum
	Sweden	- Stockholm/Esselte, Akademi Bokhandel, Fritzes, Hedengrens Gothenburg/Gumperts, Esselte Lund/Gleerupska
	Switzerland	- Easel/Bilder; Berne/Atlas; Geneve/Artou; Lausanne/Artou; Zurich/Travel Bookshop

Private buyers may also write direct to the publishers for copies to be sent by mail. The price in this instance is the retail price of the book plus postage & packing (within Britain; Continental Europe; Africa; Americas; Asia; Australasia.)

Contents

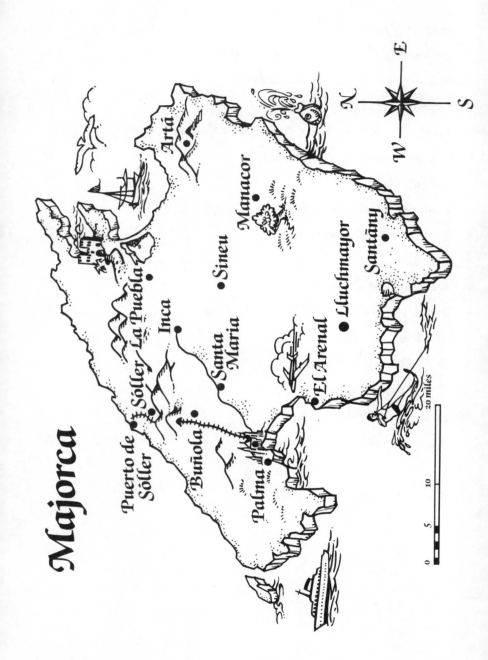

Majorca

Puerto de Sóller
Sóller
La Puebla
Inca
Buñola
Artá
Palma
Santa Maria
Sineu
Manacor
El Arenal
Lluchmayor
Santañy

N
E
W
S

0 5 10 20 miles

1. An Introduction to the Soller Railway

The cosmopolitan bustle of the tree-lined streets and plazas of Palma is just feet away, but as you mount the cast-iron steps on to the ornate riding platform of the Soller train, and sit on the hard yet perplexingly comfortable seats in the beautifully presented second-class carriages, you could be forgiven for imagining you are a million miles and a hundred years away from the intensity of twentieth-century life.

The station for trains to Soller hides away behind a pavement café in the corner of the elegant Plaza España — one of Palma's busiest squares from where public transport leaves for all parts of the island.

In the centre of the square, surrounded by half a dozen lanes of fast swirling traffic — constantly reminiscent of Trafalgar Square in the rush hour — is a small green haven with kiosks and benches for those pedestrians who fool-hardily endanger their lives by crossing the road! There to greet them is a statue of Jaime I, a name that crops up repeatedly on road and plaza names throughout the island in celebration of his conquest in 1229 over Majorca's several hundred years of domination by the Moors. Nowadays, the statue of Jaime I attracts many camera-clicking tourists and even more dirt-depositing pigeons! Proudly sitting astride his steed, perhaps Jaime deserves a little more respect...

On the same plaza is a bus station for transport to outlying villages and resorts, as well as a more local and regular service to El Arenal, the popular holiday haunt a few miles along the coast to the east of Palma, and a completely separate railway station for trains leaving for Inca. Although nearly forty years

7

older than the Soller railway, the Inca line — on which the first locomotive was brought into service on the 18-mile Palma to Inca section during the mid 1870s, reaching La Puebla by 1878 — is far less picturesque than the Soller route and operates for more practical reasons than merely a scenic journey for tourists.

At one time, not too many years ago, this state-run railway had branch lines reaching out to Manacor (opened 1879) and Arta to the north, and Felanitx (opened 1897) and Santany

Jaime I of Aragon astride his steed, still proudly watches over the land he took from the Moors during the invasion of 1229. The statue, complete with pigeons, is in the centre of Plaza España.

(opened 1917) to the east. But during the 1950s and 1960s, when freight traffic began to decline because of improvements to the island's roads, uneconomic sections of the 210km railway system were drastically cut, leaving just over 100km of the line by the mid 1970s. Today, the only remaining section of the system is the original 30km line to Inca. Tourists do use the Inca line, not so much for the scenery en route (it passes through some of Palma's poorest districts), but more as a convenient and economical way of visiting the attractive and typically Majorcan town at the end of the line.

It's quite the opposite on the Soller line, where people travel for the sheer joy of the exhilarating journey through farmland, citrus and olive groves and high up through the Alfabia mountain range. The unexpected bonus for the first-time traveller is the attractive and little-spoilt town of Soller at the end of the line, and the unique experience of travelling on the ancient tram system which connects Soller to its bustling port — nowadays a busy holiday resort — some three miles (4.8 km) away.

(Following page, top) *The tree shaded station of Soller hasn't changed since 1912. These plane trees protect passengers waiting on the 100-metre long platform from the heat of the mid-day sun.*

(Following page, bottom) *Puerto de Soller, a three-mile tram ride from its parent town, is nowadays a popular tourist resort. Before the relatively recent tourist invasion, Puerto de Soller was merely a picturesque fishing village. In past centuries there were watch posts here to give warning of potentially more devastating invasions of pirates and marauding navies of enemy nations.*

2. Soller — An Island Within an Island

The Soller railway was built at the beginning of this century for purely economic and commercial reasons, although during the past decade or so the picturesque, hour-long journey from Palma to Soller has been successfully aimed at Majorca's year round influx of visitors from all corners of the world.

The picture-postcard town of Soller, famous for its citrus groves, nestles in a valley of the same name in the mountainous north-west of the island, surrounded by Majorca's highest peaks — a situation which may seem to onlookers to be idyllic. During the latter half of the nineteenth century this unique geographical situation, which for many centuries had proved to be a major and much-envied advantage for the townsfolk of Soller, turned out to be disastrous. The town's economy began a decline due to its isolation from the rest of the island and especially from Palma, which has always been important as the island's commercial centre.

The Soller Valley is saucer-shaped and, by no accident of planning, the town sits proudly in the centre, overlooked to the north by the island's highest mountain, the 4,900-feet-high Puig Mayor. The only exits from that saucer are via a hairpin-bending (and often hair-raising!) pass to the south which twists and snakes through the mountain range, and at Puerto de Soller via a narrow opening into the sea.

As with many Mediterranean settlements, Soller was developed a few miles inland from the coast to protect it from pirate raids, with fortified watch-towers overlooking the sea acting as an early-warning system for the town. For centuries the small port bore the brunt of such attacks. In fact, so successful was the physical positioning and defence system of the town of Soller, that when Jaime I of Aragon — James the Conqueror — invaded Majorca in 1229 to overthrow the long-

---

Jaime I — ''El Conquistador''

In the thirteenth century the townsfolk of Soller were alone in successfully repelling the forces of Jaime I — King James I of Aragon. But Majorca in general owes much to ''El Conquistador'', not least of all for the massive and magnificent Gothic pile of Palma Cathedral.

The story goes that when Jaime was on his way across the 140 miles of open sea from the Spanish mainland in September 1229 to overthrow the Moorish domination of Majorca, he and his 15,000 warriors were caught up in ferocious gales. Jaime vowed that if he lived through the storms, in thanks to God he would build a cathedral on the island, dedicated to the Virgin Mary.

Weather-beaten but alive, he landed in Santa Ponsa — now a popular resort on the island's south west coast — and after three months of bloody battles, seized Palma on the last day of the year. During the ensuing year, on the site of a mosque, work was started on the cathedral to fulfil his vow.

However, Jaime missed out on seeing the completed cathedral by 300 years — main structural work finished around 1600, although additional work was carried out during the seventeenth and nineteenth centuries. And during the early years of this century, the controversial Catalan architect Antonio Gaudi — perhaps best known for his much praised, much criticised and as yet unfinished Sagrada Familia temple in Barcelona — was commissioned to remodel the interior of Palma Cathedral.

---

established Moorish domination of the island, he and his 15,000 troops never succeeded in reaching Soller.

The Soller Valley is perhaps the most fertile area of Majorca. The name, given to it by the Moors, means "The Golden Valley" or "The Golden Shell" depending on which translation you prefer. Its unique saucer shape protects the floor of the valley from winds in every direction, thus allowing tremendously varied crops — oranges, lemons, olives and almonds being amongst the most prolific — to grow in abundance. One of the most incongruous sights of the valley, depicted on picture-postcards of the area, is citrus groves with trees laden with ripe fruit, whilst in the background is the mighty Puig Mayor peak capped with glistening snow. During the months leading up to harvesting, especially in February when the area is ablaze with beautiful white almond blossom, there is an intense and delightful aroma in the town.

Soller's successfully impenetrable position meant that communications with the rest of the island were extremely difficult. However, during the nineteenth century the townsfolk overcame this problem by finding far more accessible markets for their produce — and in particular their citrus fruit — on the Mediterranean coast of France, centering around Marseilles. Business with France boomed, and after harvesting their own crops, many Soller men accompanied their produce on the sea journey to Marseilles to undertake seasonal harvesting work in France.

This economically sensible to-ing and fro-ing to France continued until relatively recent times, and it was only when Puerto de Soller began to prosper as a holiday resort in the 1940s and 1950s that the men of Soller stayed at home to develop their tourist industry.

By the end of the nineteenth century, the main business boom with the south of France began to wane, and it was then that Soller's geographical situation on the island — isolated from its potential home markets — began to be a problem rather than a much-coveted advantage. It was at this time that ambitious, and to many people absurd, initial plans

13

'Welcome to Soller' says the sign — and how about a welcoming glass of freshly squeezed orange juice in the station bar?

were drawn up to overcome the mountain barrier and to connect Soller by rail to Palma, where it was becoming obvious that the economic future of the town lay.

Today, Soller is an attractive and bustling town with a cosmopolitan atmosphere. It is not typically Majorcan, or even Spanish. Its unusual yet handsome architecture and characterful plazas and streets could well lead you to believe that you are actually in southern France. The typical cuisine of the town has a hint of Cordon Bleu and, even today, it is not uncommon to hear older residents speaking in French rather than Spanish or Mallorquin.

In the tree-shaded main square, Plaza Constitucio, with its ornamental fountain and pavement cafés and bars catering for locals rather than visitors, is the tall and awe-inspiring parish

14

church of San Bartolomé, built with an unusual, if not ugly, art nouveau style of facade. Inside there are two splendid statues — one of the patron saint, St Bartholomew carved in black marble, and the other a beautiful fourteenth-century Madonna.

To cater for the visitor, shops on Calle de la Luna, the main street leading off the square, offer an extensive range of locally-produced ceramics and hand-carved olive-wood souvenirs, whilst an occasional market in a small square to the rear of the church offers mainly household wares and clothing for the local residents, but is nonetheless worthy of a visit.

One of the most picturesque buildings in the town is Soller railway station, originally built in 1606 as a stage-coach station. Developed as the town's railway station in 1910, it is situated in Plaza España, from where trains leave for Palma and the old tram begins its slow trundle to Puerto de Soller, only three miles (4.8 km) yet more than half-an-hour's rickety ride away. The tranquil station also boasts one of Soller's finest restaurants, known not only for its excellent food, but also for its early twentieth-century Parisian style of decor.

3. Puerto de Soller — From Fishing Port to Major Resort

There was a time when Puerto de Soller was no more than a collection of fishermen's hovels and fortified look-out posts around a large sheltered circular bay, with a narrow opening leading to the sea. But times change, and today Puerto de Soller is amongst the most popular holiday resorts on Majorca, attracting thousands of English, German and French tourists each year.

The tourist invasion has brought with it employment and wealth for the inhabitants, as well as the development of many luxury hotels and sophisticated restaurants and night clubs. In fact, nowadays, Puerto de Soller is a major conurbation in its own right rather than just the port and access to the sea for the main town of Soller; and it is almost certainly far more prosperous — and if restaurant prices are anything to go by, far more expensive — than its parent town three miles away. The Soller to Puerto de Soller tramway is now well and truly established as a major tourist attraction. From Soller, the vintage tramcars rattle their way through farmyards and citrus groves until they reach the coast road. The track then follows the entire sweep of the bay, and passes the fishing fleet jetties, sea front cafés, hotels and shops before completing its picturesque and leisurely journey at the Puerto terminus.

4. A Commitment to Communicate

Throughout their long and, in the main, successful history, the people of Soller have always been proud of their town and of their accomplishments. When faced with adversity, they have invariably worked together to overcome their problems in order to prosper.

At the end of the nineteenth century, the 9,000 inhabitants of Soller were faced with three alternatives:

— to continue in the status-quo, but risk the strong possibility of rapid economic decline, if not poverty;

— to follow many of their forefathers and emigrate to Southern France or to the Spanish mainland in order to survive and prosper;

— or to establish, very quickly, much improved communications with the rest of the island so they could take advantage of potential home markets and the commercial facilities of Palma.

Needless to say the last choice was adopted by the majority. In 1899 several plans were drawn up to replace the existing hazardous mountain track with a proper road through the mountains to connect Soller with Palma, yet enormous technical problems meant that these ideas had to be shelved and that the planners had to consider the possible alternatives.

Four years later, in March 1903, the town council of Soller

(Following page) *San Bartolomé Parish Church, tall and awe-inspiring with its art nouveau facade, overshadows the pavement cafés of Soller's main square, Plaza Constitucio.*

discussed the possibility of burrowing a long railway tunnel through the mountain range, but problems arose again when even the experts brought in to advise on the scheme were not willing to project the possible financial cost of overcoming the major difficulties encompassed within the plan.

At about the same time, an elaborate plan was being drawn up for the whole of Majorca and the smaller Balearic islands which, amongst other things, allowed handsome subsidies for the construction of railways which spanned 18.5 miles (29.6 km) or more. Because the proposed line from Soller to Palma was to measure just 17 miles (27.2 km), it did not automatically qualify. Nevertheless, at a session of the Soller town council, held on 20 September 1904, it was agreed that the Majorcan public authorities should be pressed to include the proposed railway in their overall plan for the island and that a deadline should be set for the commencement of work.

The council had the full support of industry and commerce from the whole of Majorca for their railway plan, and eventually it was due to the intervention and support of the much-respected Majorcan-born statesman and former Prime Minister of Spain, Antonio Maura, that the plans received official blessing. The news was received with great enthusiasm and the people of Soller held a series of celebrations.

(Following page, top) *The station entrance in Palma is an elegant legacy of the early 1900s when Ferrocarril de Soller started its first regular service from Soller through the mountains to Palma.*

(Following page, bottom) *This Inca bound train stands at the railway station on the other side of Plaza España and serves passengers travelling to the middle of the island. The service, first opened in the mid-1870s, has been modernised with less characterful rolling stock than that which operates on the Soller route.*

Antonio Maura

Without the intervention of Antonio Maura, it is doubtful that the Soller to Palma railway would exist today. Born in Palma in May 1853, Maura was five times Prime Minister of Spain. He was educated in Palma and Madrid and graduated in law.

Maura was elected to the Cortes — the Spanish parliament — in 1881 and his first senior post was as Minister for the Colonies in 1892. Three years later he was appointed Minister of Justice, and in 1902 he became Minister of the Interior.

Maura led a breakaway Liberal group which eventually joined the Conservative Party, and he first became Prime Minister in December 1903. During his second term of office (1907-1909) he succeeded in reforming local government and the election process — ridding it of corruption and abuse. He was also responsible for making education compulsory throughout Spain.

Under pressure in 1912, Maura resigned his seat in parliament and his position as leader of the Conservative Party. However, he headed three more short-lived national governments in 1913, 1919 and 1921. Although actively disliked by the opposition parties because of his strongly-held right-wing attitudes, Maura was a highly-respected statesman and scholar and was elected director of the Royal Spanish Academy. He died in 1925 at the age of 72.

Once the euphoria had died down, the serious work of carrying the plans a step further had to commence. In October 1904, engineer Pedro Garau was appointed by Soller town council and given the task of producing a detailed blueprint for the railway's construction.

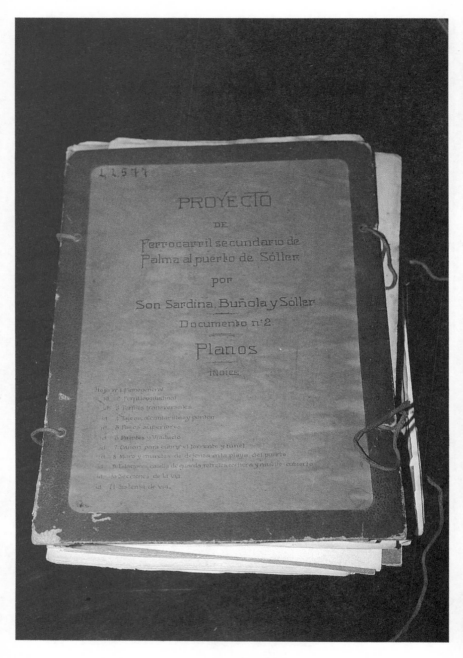

Pedro Garau's original blue-print for the construction of the Soller to Palma railway. The historic document is kept at Soller Station under lock and key.

Within a month, he had completed his initial drawings in which he proposed that the Soller to Palma railway should cross the daunting natural obstacle of the Alfabia Mountains by means of a three-kilometre-long tunnel blasted through the rock. Once the people of Soller had been convinced that this would be technically possible, and not merely a theoretical drawing, the town welcomed the Garau blueprint with great enthusiasm and celebrated the fact that, at long last, a definite plan for their railway had been produced.

The estimated cost of the total project was a little under 3,150,000 pesetas (by today's exchange rate, less than £18,000!), which averaged out at around 116,650 pesetas for each of the line's 27 kilometres. This envisaged cost had to be met to a great extent by the 9,000 people of Soller. But once again the town's inhabitants worked together to overcome the financial problem — after all, it had taken many years to get this far with their railway plan, so they were not going to let finance stand in the way now.

In July 1905, a committee was formed charged with the total responsibility of the railway's finance, construction and ultimate usage. Seven thousand railway company shares were issued, each valued at 500 pesetas, and within a very short time all the necessary cash had been raised. Shareholders included not only rich merchants who had invested many thousands of pesetas, but also some of the poorest people of the town who were eager to be part of the exciting venture.

The Garau blueprint was given official government approval in March 1907, and at the end of the following month the contract for tunnelling and construction work was put out to tender. After much competition, the contract was won by Luis Bovio who indicated that the work would take two years and ten months to complete.

5. Under the Mountains to Palma

Construction work began on 3 June 1907, and just twenty days later, drilling started on the main three-kilometre-long tunnel which was to take the railway line under the mountains. On 23 August 1910, Constanza Gamazo — wife of project enthusiast Antonio Maura — was given the honour, in front of many local dignitaries and crowds of Soller people, of firing the final blast which would complete the giant hole through the mountain range.

Meanwhile, back in 1908, the company of Ferrocarril de Soller was officially formed and was granted the sole concession for the operation of a railway line between Palma and Puerto de Soller. Modifications to the initial Palma/Soller railway blueprint were therefore made to incorporate a 4.8 kilometre extension to the line, between Soller and its port. The designated budget for the railway was also revised to reflect the additional work, and the new total cost was put at just under four and a half million pesetas. It was also agreed at this time that the traction for the main Soller-Palma line was to be of steam and the Soller-Puerto de Soller extension — although of the same three-feet track gauge as the main line — should be electric, powering motorised tram-type coaches.

In the final reckoning, the cash actually invested in Ferrocarril de Soller was five and a half million pesetas — three and a half million of which was raised through shares and the remainder in loans payable over 80 years. The original budget had therefore suffered an increase of more than 75 per cent.

With tunnelling successfully completed, the positioning and

TUNNELS OF THE PALMA/SOLLER RAILWAY

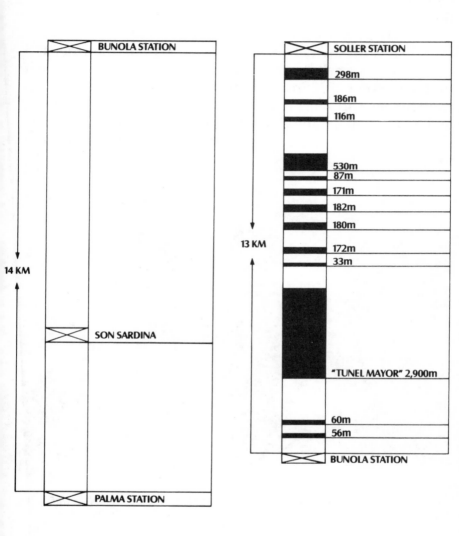

BUNOLA STATION

SON SARDINA

PALMA STATION

14 KM

SOLLER STATION

298m
186m
116m

530m
87m
171m
182m
180m

172m
33m

"TUNEL MAYOR" 2,900m

60m
56m

BUNOLA STATION

13 KM

25

laying of the track started at the beginning of April 1911. Work began at Palma and the line reached Soller station six months later. Once the track had been laid as far as the northern end of the major tunnel, the contractor organised a celebratory trip along the first seventeen kilometres of track from Palma for the railway company's board of directors and other VIPs. A small steam engine named "Maria Luisa", built in Loughborough, England twenty years previously, was used for the trip. This engine normally transported labourers and equipment up and down the line, and its historic journey on 25 July 1911 received much acclaim from the public and press alike.

The No 1 Steam Locomotive "Soller" which pulled the first complete train on the entirety of the route in March 1912 - one month before the line was officially opened. "Soller" continued in service until the line was electrified in 1929.

On 11 October, one week after the completion of track laying, the honour was bestowed upon Antonio Maura to make the official inaugural rail journey from Palma all the way to Soller. The trip was made by again using the Maria Luisa engine, but with coaches loaned for the occasion by Ferrocarril de Mallorca, the company which operated the already existing Palma-Inca line.

At the beginning of March 1912, a Spanish-built steam engine, christened "Palma", was put to test on the line. During the following few weeks two more locomotives and several passenger and freight carriages, constructed in Zaragoza on the Spanish mainland by the company Carde and Escoriaza, came into service. In the middle of March a complete train, its freight and passenger coaches pulled by the Number One engine appropriately called "Soller", underwent successful trials on the entire length of the line.

With many years of dedicated hard work and months of trials now complete, the Soller to Palma railway was being acclaimed as Spain's finest transport system.

6. The Great Day Dawns

On 16 April 1912, the day finally arrived for the official opening of the line. The town councils of Palma, Bunola and Soller joined forces for the ceremony, with thousands of happy onlookers from all over the island. The official train, with all the company's coaches pulled by the engines "Soller" and "Palma", left the capital with many VIPs at 3.05pm to the cheers and applause of crowds who had gathered at the station and surrounding areas. Such was the jubilation and enthusiasm of the crowds at Son Sardina and Bunola that the train had to stop whilst huge numbers of cheering spectators were cleared from the line.

Newspaper reports of the occasion, perhaps using a little journalistic licence, claimed that Soller's total population, young and old, had gone to "their" station to greet "their" train and to cheer "their" railway. These people, after all, had made huge sacrifices and invested the best part of their life savings to make what seemed an impossible dream come true.

The Bishop of Majorca celebrated the occasion with a blessing at which all company personnel and shareholders were present. Tributes were paid to the many people whose tireless endeavours and skilful work had made the venture possible, and specific praise was given to Sr Garau for his initial railway blueprint, and to the many distinguished people whose work, both individually and collectively, was said to have been oustanding.

Unfortunately the opening of the Soller-Puerto de Soller section could not coincide with the "big day" because work on the track and the overhead electric power supply was yet to be finished. The work continued until September 1913 when construction was complete, electricity sub-stations had been built and tram-type motorised coaches and accompanying carriages had been delivered by manufacturers Carde and Escoriaza. Trials on the 4,868 metre-long section were carried out with excellent results at the end of September and the official opening of the service was held on 11 October when, once again, dignitaries and officials from all over the island gathered in Soller to celebrate the inaugural trip of Majorca's first-ever tram. At the official opening, the Bishop of Majorca blessed the motorised coaches and carriages — so well that most of them are still in regular use to this day!

The Official Opening Day Photograph of important personalities gathered for the occasion on April 16 1912. This picture includes: Statesman and project enthusiast Antonio Maura; his wife Constanza Gamazo - who two years previously was given the privilege of firing the final charge to complete the boring of Tunel Mayor; and Pedro Garau who prepared the working plans for the construction of the line.

An Historic Day

Tuesday 16 April 1912 saw history in the making for Majorca with the official opening of Ferrocarril de Soller. But the world's press was pre-occupied with more devastating news about transport. It was on that very day when the news broke that the world's largest and most luxurious ship, the *Titanic*, had collided with an iceberg in the Atlantic during her maiden voyage.

The liner — the jewel in the crown of the White Star Line — had left Southampton for New York on the previous Wednesday. Five days into her voyage, in the vicinity of the Newfoundland banks, south of Cape Race, the ill-fated *Titanic* struck the iceberg. Although the initial news reports of 16 April stated that all 2,200 passengers and crew were safe, within 48 hours it became horribly apparent that the "unsinkable" 46,000 ton ship, which had cost an unprecedented £1.5 million to build, had taken with her to the ocean bed more than 1,500 souls.

The Daily Mirror

THE MORNING JOURNAL WITH THE SECOND LARGEST NET SALE.

No. 2,645.   Registered at the G.P.O. as a Newspaper.   TUESDAY, APRIL 16, 1912   One Halfpenny

DISASTER TO THE TITANIC: WORLD'S LARGEST SHIP COLLIDES WITH AN ICEBERG IN THE ATLANTIC DURING HER MAIDEN VOYAGE.

7. Running Out of Steam

During the period 1913 to 1929, the life of Ferrocarril de Soller, both on the railway and the tramway, developed relatively normally. However, wear and tear on equipment and the rising cost of maintenance, renewal and replacement — compounded by a campaign against the increasing of fares — meant that within a few years the company was operating at a loss, with no benefit to shareholders.

Then, in 1924, a new statute was approved for Ferrocarril de Soller, and the company's managing director at the time, Jeronimo Estades, won a personal triumph in obtaining permission from the Spanish Caretaker of Railways for his line to be electrified. A budget of 2,209,000 pesetas was made available for the work.

The plan presented was the work of engineer Juan Frontera, and was given official blessing by the Spanish railways authority during July 1926.

(Opposite) *Coupling up. This man has the responsible job of connecting two passenger carriages. He must connect and tension the coupling grapple to join the carriages, ensure that the buffers are just touching to keep them apart and, finally, lock together the vital airhoses which power the brakes on this tortuous line.*

(Top) *The town of Soller sits proudly in the centre of a large geological saucer surrounded - and during the past thousand years protected - by the Alfabia mountain range. To the north, Soller is overlooked by Puig Mayor - at 4,900 feet, Majorca's highest peak.*

(Above) *The ticket hall at Soller seen as one descends from the platform. Built in 1606 as a coaching stage, the well, which was originally used to water the horses, has been retained for its historical association.*

Shaded sidings at Soller. A tranquil end to a spectacular journey.

The inauguration of the electrified services was held on 4 July 1929, when numerous dignitaries, shareholders and members of the public attended an official ceremony. Yet deficiencies in construction resulted in the steam service continuing until 1 November, by which time problems had been sorted out and everything was functioning perfectly. The steam engines were replaced by four 33-ton, wooden-built electric motor coaches, all of which are still in regular service today.

For many years after the electrification of the line, the future of Ferrocarril de Soller looked uncertain, owing to rising costs of overheads and the ever-reducing number of people actually using the service. Much improved road communications also meant that the railway's freight traffic dwindled. But the tourist invasion of Majorca during the past twenty years has given the service a new lease of life, to a point where nowadays one has to be at the station a long time before scheduled departure to ensure a seat in the first-class compartment. Throughout the year, at least five journeys are made in each direction every day, with more on Sundays and festival days.

Until the sun stops shining on Majorca and the tourists no longer visit the island, the 100 employees working for the only privately-owned railway company in Spain seem to be guaranteed a secure job!

(Opposite) *Modern passenger car interior. Reversible leatherette seats provide seating for 52 passengers.*

(Following page) *Electric Locomotive No 3, one of the original wooden clad models of 1929. The motors were manufactured by Siemens in Germany and the body work was built by Carde & Escoriaza in Zaragoza, Spain. Each locomotive is powered by four 120-hp motors with current from 1200-volt DC overhead cables. Each locomotive weighs 33 tons and has seating capacity for 44 passengers.*

8. Palma to Soller
— The Enchanting Route

Three rings on the 75-year-old brass bell on the station wall, a shrill blast on the station-master's hand-held bugle, answered by two short hoots by the train-driver, indicate that the train is about to start its hour-long, 27-kilometre journey through the mountains from Palma to Soller.

The 60-year old wooden-built electric engine — itself carrying some 30 second-class passengers on beautifully preserved high-backed slatted wooden seats, and twelve first-class passengers in the unashamed luxury of individual padded armchairs — creaks its way slowly out of Palma station, pulling five elegant wooden carriages, each capable of seating up to 52 enthusiastic travellers.

Because of the favourable year-round climate, but most of all because of the uniquely scenic mountain route of the train, many passengers choose to stand for the duration of the journey on the exterior cast-iron ornate riding platforms at each end of every carriage. The favourite position is, of course, the platform at the rear of the train. Standing there, one can imagine the nineteenth-century experience of rail travel in the Wild West, picking off Red Indians or outlaws as they attempt to raid the train.

Many of the carriages used today date back to the early years of this century when the Ferrocarril de Soller Palma/Soller railway was first opened. They are superbly maintained and original in every detail, including solid brass swivel wall fittings to take candles to illuminate the carriage whilst travelling through tunnels under the Alfabia Mountain range. Since 1929, however, the track has been electrified so these fittings are now purely a splendid legacy and wonderful reminder of an elegant, long-gone era.

Leaving Palma

On its three-foot gauge track, the gentle giant slowly leaves the long, narrow platform of Palma station and passes through huge iron gates, leaving behind it a peaceful sanctuary in the middle of what seems to be a city of endless and exciting pandemonium. From the station compound, the track takes the train into the centre of Calle Eusebio Estaba, the main road leading north from Plaza España to the city's suburbs. Immediately to the right is the vast and rather featureless railway compound, sidings and station of Ferrocarril de Mallorca from where trains leave for Inca.

The Power of a Woman. With the wave of her hand this policewoman can stop the train as it moves along the street in the first section of its 17-mile journey to Soller.

As the train snakes its way at a slow walking pace up the centre of the road, it quite often hits Palma's seemingly perpetual rush hour and is held up at traffic signals and through the mad antics of buses, vans, cars and the impatient drivers of the city's taxis. And Palma must be one of the very few places in the world where traffic police on point duty in the middle of the road have it in their power to wave on or, at their discretion, bring to a halt several hundred tons of railway train!

Houses, flats, shops and business premises overlook the track on either side of the road, and as the train goes through road junctions and traffic lights, it hoots to warn motorists not to argue with it. At fourteen minutes into the journey, the track leaves the centre of the road and follows its own right of way between tenement blocks in one of Palma's poorest, scruffiest and most litter-strewn suburbs. But soon this visual pollution passes and a pungent odour penetrates the nostrils as we travel within feet of the stable blocks of Palma's hippodrome, where visitors who want a little flutter can lose their favourite Hawaiian shirt on the regular horse-and-trap races.

The journey then takes us through one of Palma's sprawling industrial quarters, and the smell of horse manure is swapped for the rather more pleasant odour of frying as we pass the "007" potato crisp factory and the complementary Aguila beer plant. On the left we pass a furniture storage warehouse, a power station and the Roca factory — one of Spain's leading bathroom equipment manufacturers. Just a couple of minutes later, after passing the first open countryside of the route, we arrive at Son Sardina — the tiniest of hamlets which boasts its own station on the Palma to Soller line. By British standards, the station is so small that it could easily pass as an elaborate bus-shelter!

Crossing the Plain

Immediately after re-starting the journey from Son Sardina, we almost converge with the main Palma-Soller road which is running absolutely parallel with the track, some 20 metres to the left. We are now travelling on the Plain of Majorca, surrounded by thousand upon thousand of ancient olive trees. There is little development here apart from the odd smallholding growing everything from vines to cabbages, one or two modern villas complete with large, landscaped gardens and swimming pools, and, on the right, a completely deserted, camouflage-painted military base. Looking back, a trained eye can pick out landmark buildings of Palma in the distance; look to the left or forwards, and you can see the mountains which form the west-coast spine of Majorca, from the furthest point south to the furthest point north. But adjacent to the track are extensive flat fields of trees, some with sheep and goats grazing, and some with almost derelict, yet still occupied, homesteads.

Into the Hills

At thirty minutes into the journey the world begins to look a little more rugged as we pass terraces of citrus and olive trees and, on the right, steep embankments about twice as high as the train carriages. The train perceptibly slows down as it struggles up a slight gradient leading into the quaint station of Bunola, the town which is almost exactly the half-way point between Palma and Soller.

Bunola station is absolutely appropriate for the village it serves — sleepy, pretty and disturbingly quiet and still at all times other than when a train rattles through. At the side of the railway line are piled hundreds of hefty wooden sleepers and lengths of rusting rail, presumably used as spares, though, judging by the flora established amongst them, they may well have been there since the opening of the route in 1912.

The village of Bunola lies about half a mile up a steep, leafy road from the station, but is well worth the hike. The village

Bunola Station half a kilometre north of the halfway point of the journey. It is within a kilometre north of Bunola that the train enters the first of thirteen tunnels on the route.

centre is no more than a handful of shops, bars and white houses clustered around an old Gothic church and a sheltered paved square where the lined and leather-faced old men of the community congregate to exchange gossip and doze under the hot sun. For the few passengers who venture off the train to visit Bunola, the village comes as a refreshing change to the comparative hustle and bustle of Palma and, to a lesser extent, Soller. Prices, for instance, in the somewhat less sophisticated bars of the sleepy village are a fraction of those in the island's capital. In fact the only evidence of the twentieth century in Bunola are a few battered and carelessly-parked ''Seats'' and a couple of telephone booths which claim to be able to cope with both national and international calls. Very few village inhabitants are cosmopolitan enough to put that claim to the test!

The First Tunnels

After a blast on the station-master's bugle, the train leaves Bunola station and negotiates a long, left-hand curve which leads to the first of the route's thirteen tunnels — an insignificant 56 metres long. The straight Palma to Soller road still runs parallel to the track about 200 metres to the left, across fields where sheep graze amongst the almond and olive trees. After passing through another tunnel of 60 metres in length, the train begins a noticeably steep ascent of about one in forty before — at 38 minutes into the journey — disappearing from the brilliant and warm sunlight on the Palma side of the mountains into the third and longest tunnel of the route — the 2,900 metre long "Tunel Mayor".

The Longest Tunnel

The construction of Tunel Mayor proved to be the most expensive and most problematical of the total railway system. Blasting and drilling on the three-kilometre-long hole through the mountains began in June 1907 and it was more than three years later, at the end of August 1910, when the hole finally had two ends and became a tunnel.

Although the train takes just five and a half minutes to pass through Tunel Mayor, they seem the longest five and a half minutes of the whole one-hour long journey. The clatter of the wheels and the noise of the engine is quite deafening; the carriages are dimly lit by insufficient wattage, and the air temperature drops dramatically. Looking out of the window, the train appears to be travelling at an incredible rate, but this is purely an illusion brought about by the rough, black, wet walls of the tunnel allowing just four or five inches of clearance for the sides of the train. In Tunel Mayor you put your head out of the window or hang over the safety rail of the riding platform at your own risk ... and be careful not to lose your head!

At forty minutes into the journey, it is a pleasure to leave the dank hell of Tunel Mayor and reappear in the bright mountain sunshine. During the next few minutes, that sunshine is only interrupted by, first, a "mini" tunnel of just 33 metres and then two more tunnels, each of a little under 200 metres in length. Now the track almost converges with the often precarious Palma to Soller road which winds its way up, through and down the mountain range by a seemingly endless series of ultra-tight hairpin bends. The road is perhaps one reason why the train journey is so popular; it is certainly not for the inexperienced or timid driver!

Tunnel Vision. A train may be seen approaching through the far tunnel. The near tunnel is the first on the route encountered shortly after Bunola Station.

Tourist Stop

Once through the next tunnel, the train comes to a halt at the specially-constructed "tourist stop" at which certain trains during the day stop for eight or nine minutes to allow passengers to get off to take in their first breathtaking views of the whole of the Golden Valley of Soller. More photographs are taken at this point of the route than any other — and quite rightly so.

The panorama is so stunning that it seems unreal — Soller, in the centre of the valley, appears like a fairy-tale village hundreds of feet below, surrounded by majestic mountains reaching into the fluffy white clouds.

A couple of hoots from the engine tell the passengers to return to their seats and off chugs the train to continue the last part of its journey.

Time for passengers to stretch their legs and test their telephoto lenses at the "tourist stop", high up in the mountains.

Two more tunnels — at 171 metres and 87 metres respectively — and the train crosses a completely symmetrical five-arch viaduct, ingeniously built over a 50-metre-wide valley in the mountains. Constructed during the first few years of this century in the remote mountains and without the aid of today's high-tech machinery, this viaduct must surely be one of the most extraordinary feats of engineering and architecture of its era.

The "U-Turn" Tunnel

With just ten minutes until the train reaches its final destination, passengers are now accustomed to the sight of Soller way below them to the right. But the next two minutes succeed in disorientating all unsuspecting, first-time travellers. The train now enters the tenth and, at 530 metres, the second longest tunnel of the route. Imperceptibly, the train goes through a 180 degree curve in its mountain climb during the 530 metres of this tunnel. So when it finally exits

Permanent Way Gang being towed to work by a passenger train.

from the darkness, the town of Soller takes everyone by surprise lying several hundred feet down ... on the left!

Alongside the track are expertly terraced fields which allow the farmers to grow their crops on the flat, each terrace having an abundance of centuries-old gnarled olive trees and fruit-laden lemon and orange trees. Much of the rock and infill for the more recent terraces was provided courtesy of the railway company — until the early 1900s when holes were blasted in mountains to form tunnels, it had lain undisturbed for millions of years.

After reappearing from two more tunnels — of 116 metres and 186 metres — passengers have a superb view over the whole of the town of Soller. But dominating the scene, with the town's highest buildings and church towers silhouetted against it, is Puig Mayor — at 4,900 feet, the island's highest peak. Its summit, which during the winter months is quite often capped with snow, is normally hidden amongst the clouds.

At fifty-six minutes into the journey, passengers experience the last of the route's thirteen tunnels which altogether account for almost five kilometres of the total distance of the track. Once again, the brass and wooden fittings in the carriages glisten in the dim electric light and the noise becomes so intense that you cannot hear yourself speak. And again, from 70 or 80 degrees of sunshine, the temperature drops at least 20 degrees (10°C) in the cool, dank darkness of this 298 metre-long tunnel. But then, with a little more than two minutes to go, the train reappears in the daylight for its final descent into Soller.

(Opposite) *The symmetrical, five-arch viaduct which carries the track 50 metres across a valley in the Alfabia Mountains north of the Tunel Mayor.*

44

45

Emerging into the sunlight a Palma bound train passes out of one of the routes 13 tunnels.

Driver's view of the final approach into the Soller Station area. The buildings on the left are the engine sheds for both the 36" gauge railway locomotives and trams.

Down Into Soller

Although the train is making a tremendous noise as it crawls down its iron hill, the sheep, goats, donkeys and poultry behind the wire fencing, separating the gardens and smallholdings from the track, completely ignore us and continue their munchings amongst the lemon trees. After all, some ten trains a day, seven days per week pass within a few feet of their habitat, so they are quite used to the racket and bored with excited passengers shooting them (...at f11 at 500th of a second).

And then after an hour's journey through the Sierra Norte — the northern part of the Alfabia mountain range which for centuries proved to be a natural and inconquerable barrier between the beautiful golden valley of Soller and the rest of the island of Majorca — the train finally chugs through the fifteen-feet-wide opening between engine sheds and workshops to enter the leafy and mellow environs of Soller

The Director's Railcar. This fascinating rail-wheeled car was built in 1917 by the Renault Company in France. No museum piece, this vehicle is used regularly by the managing director for inspection purposes and is photographed here at the popular tourist stop which overlooks the Soller Valley.

station where the passengers disembark after their enchanting journey.

Inside the engine sheds and workshops in the station compound is a railway enthusiast's wonderland. Serving not only the train engines and carriages but also the ancient trams which rattle their meandering way between Soller and its port, the sheds contain some magnificently maintained and preserved hardware dating back to the turn of the century. The *pièce de résistance* is perhaps the railway company managing director's personal train — a green, petrol driven four-seater "car" built in 1917 by the French Renault company, which, apart from its four small railway track wheels, has a remarkable resemblance to a vintage road vehicle. And, like so much of the railway company's equipment, this museum piece is not kept for purely sentimental reasons — it is used on a regular weekly basis by the managing director to inspect the line through the mountains.

(Top) *Station-master's view of a locomotive approaching the terminal platform at Soller.*

(Above) *Engine No 3 shunts out of Soller Station to collect its coaches before making its one-hour journey through the mountains to Palma.*

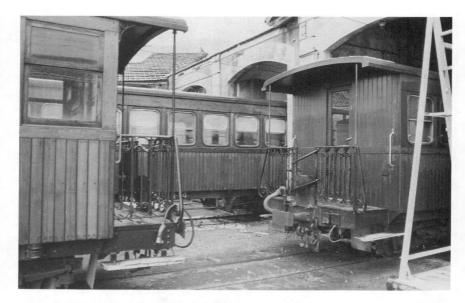

(Top) *Ornate riding platforms seldom seen in mainland Europe today provide popular vantage points. Since the advent of electric locomotives in 1929 passengers no longer suffer from the nuisance of smuts in the eye from the engines.*

(Above) *Two class locomotive car interior. This photograph shows the first class (soft) upholstered seating in the foreground with the second class (hard) slatted seating in the background.*

The Track and Hardware

The length of the route from Palma to Soller is 27.264 km, of which 22.276 km of track is in the open and 4.988 km in tunnels. The original track used was in twelve metre lengths and weighed 22.70 kilograms per metre, but following renovations much of the track is now of heftier 32 kilograms per metre. The rail gauge (distance between rails) is 0.914 metres — i.e. three feet.

All the tunnels on the route are five metres wide and 4.70 metres high. Palma station lies 24.60 metres above sea-level and, soon after leaving "Tunel Mayor", the track reaches its highest point of 240 metres above sea-level before starting its zig-zag descent into Soller at a gradient of around 1 in 43.

Ferrocarril de Soller has four "Siemens" electric engines, each powered by four 120 horse-power motors, supplied by 1200 volts d.c. from overhead cables. The wooden-built engines were constructed by Carde and Escoriaza and entered service in 1929 when the line was electrified. Each engine weighs 33 tons and has a passenger seating capacity of 44.

The original wooden-built coaches are still used on the route. Each has two bogies of two axles and weighs thirteen tons. Number One carriage has 32 first-class seats, Numbers Two and Nine have 39 seats and the rest have 52 second-class seats. Five newer carriages, modelled on the originals, entered service in 1978, each having 52 seats.

In 1968, Ferrocarril de Soller took delivery of a diesel locomotive. Powered by a Deutz motor, this 31-ton steel-bodied engine is housed in the sheds at Soller station and brought into service whenever there are problems with the electricity supply.

Three brake vans, built by Carde and Escoriaza in 1932, are used to carry mail. The 13-ton vans also have the luxury of toilet facilities. There are also around 30 freight trucks of varying sizes and open and enclosed designs.

9. From Soller to the Port — By Tram

On first appearance, the wooden-built, orange-fronted vintage trams of Soller look far too frail to do anything but stand as a proud exhibit in some transport museum. They certainly do not seem capable of carrying passengers at half-hourly intervals throughout the day on the three-mile trip between Soller and Puerto de Soller. But this is exactly what they have done for 75 years or more, and, by all accounts, they are set to do the same for many years to come.

Most of the original trams were built by Carde and Escoriaza on the Spanish mainland and came into service when the Soller-Puerto track was first opened in 1913. They were not shipped over from San Francisco, California, as some Majorca guide books might lead you to believe.

The Journey

From the sheds and workshops within the station compound at Soller, the tram creaks its way down the three-foot gauge track, exits through the station gates and stops at its first official pick-up point in Plaza España — immediately outside the railway station's imposing main public entrance.

Two tugs by the conductor on the bell cord which runs along the ceiling of the tram engine and its carriages, and off we go, passing a fountain and the town's taxi rank on the left and a variety of shops, banks and cafés on the right. Fifty yards further on and the tram passes gracefully through Soller's main square, Plaza Constitucio, alongside the tall church of San Bartolomé. Before joining its own right of way — a narrow strip of land between gardens and farms — the

The Soller Tram has a distinctive brown and orange livery and Cyclopic headlight. The pantograph (through an early design) replaces the traditional trolley pole.

Passing by the Church of San Bartolomé in central Soller two minutes into its journey to the port.

tram trundles along the middle of the town's main shopping street, causing traffic chaos as it passes Soller's indoor fruit market.

For about ten minutes of the half-hour, 4.8 km journey, the tram rattles its passengers along a track within arm's reach of laden citrus trees, and within a few feet of small-holdings over-populated by goats, sheep, hens and geese. The track follows the course of a wide but shallow stream which it eventually crosses via a rickety bridge. After a warning ''hoot'' it goes over a couple of side roads and then, at a snail's pace, joins the main Soller/Puerto road near to its junction with roads branching off to Palma (32km, so says the sign), Pollensa (52km) and Lluch (34km). A fourth signpost outside the Restaurante Monumento, says ''Puerto — 2km''.

The track now runs along the overgrown side of the road, again with citrus groves at arm's reach to the left. At no time does the tram exceed 15 or 16 miles per hour — perhaps a good thing considering it has little, if any, form of suspension. It has been known for it to be overtaken by donkey carts, fully laden with vegetables, on their way to market!

About to cross one of the several side roads the tram sounds its distinctive high-pitched hooter before passing into the countryside and parallel with the road between town and port.

After a few more minutes of bone-shaking, the tram comes to a halt at a passing-loop. This is a layby, where the first tram to arrive in either direction on the single line waits for the oncoming tram to pass. Surprisingly, the two trams travelling on the single-track line in opposite directions usually meet at the passing-loop within a minute or two of each other. However, drivers do occasionally spend anxious moments if one arrives very late.

Once out of the passing-loop, the tram continues its way along the side of the road towards the port. Lean out of the open-sided "Jardinera" carriages too far and you are whipped by over- growing weeds, brambles and tree branches. Over to the left is the Hotel Rocamar, and as the tram passes the "Puerto de Soller" sign at about 20 minutes into the journey, the land around the road becomes more developed with old farm houses and new villas, all covered with creeping flowers in vigorous shades of red, yellow and deep purple.

The tram now stops outside the Hostel Primavera to pick up and let down passengers, and then, very soon, joins the semi-circular sweep of the bay. The track is sandwiched between the road and the sand and shingle beach of Puerto de Soller just inches to the left. The journey round the bay to the tram's ultimate destination takes seven or eight minutes, passing, on the right, a succession of hotels, apartment blocks, shops, bars, medical centres, car-hire offices, restaurants and banks. On the left is a magnificent view of the glistening, calm blue water of the almost-enclosed bay.

We pass jetties for fishing and pleasure boats, and, during most months of the year, sunbathers stretched out on the shingle of the sheltered beach.

Turn-of-the-Century Technology

The Company's three nine-ton "Siemens" tram engines — brought into service in 1913 — are powered by two 35 horse-power electric motors, supplied by 600 volts from overhead cables. They each have a capacity for 18 seated passengers, but more often than not, a further twenty or more are carried standing up. A fourth tram engine, powered by two 37 horse-power A.E.G. electric motors and weighing in at eight tons, was acquired from northern Spain's "Tranvias de Bilbao" and entered service in 1958.

The open-sided "Jardinera" carriages, each weighing five tons and seating 24 passengers, were brought into service on the Soller/Puerto line in 1956, having been acquired from "Tranvias de Palma" — Palma's old tramway system.

For winter months, three six-ton enclosed carriages are used — two of which started life in 1913 as the Company's original hardware, and a third which Ferrocarril de Soller also bought from the Bilbao Tram Company in 1958.

A crowded tram waiting at the passing loop half-way between the town and port of Soller, for the oncoming tram.

Even though trams have plied their way along this route for more than three-quarters of a century, they still attract dozens of camera-clickers on every journey. Cars suddenly come to a halt in the centre of the road and out jumps someone armed with a camera. People quietly sitting at bars on the sea-front see the tram trundling towards them and suddenly decide to desert their drink in favour of a snap. If the tram drivers received a peseta for every photograph taken of them, they could retire as very rich men!

After another exhilarating few minutes along the water's edge, the tram completes its journey adjacent to the port's large main jetty to which are moored dozens of fishing boats of all sizes, together with pleasure craft, glass-bottomed boats and private luxury yachts and cruisers. This is the hub of Puerto de Soller where all the best (or, at least the most expensive) fish restaurants and bars are clustered around the characterful fishermen's wharf.

To end its journey, the tram stops at another passing-loop for all the remaining passengers to disembark. The conductor uncouples the motorised section from the carriages and the nine-ton engine then manoeuvres around the carriages and couples up again at the other end, ready for the return journey to the main town of Soller.

(Top) *Tram and carriage making their way along the palmtree lined waterfront at Puerto de Soller.*

(Above) *Journey's End. The Puerto de Soller seafront terminus at the end of the 4.8km journey from Soller Station. There is generally time for a drink at one of the nearby bars before starting the return journey.*

10. A Regular Service

From the station in the corner of Plaza España, Palma, Ferrocarril de Soller run five trains per day, seven days per week on the 17-mile journey to Soller.

For "first-timers", the 10.40am train — although perhaps the most crowded — is undoubtedly the one to go for. It is this train which makes a "tourist stop" to allow passengers to disembark and admire the breath-taking views from high up in the mountains across the Soller Valley and the town of Soller itself.

One word of warning: it is very easy to become stranded in Soller. For some reason, best known to the management of the railway company, if you miss the 2.10pm return train from Soller to Palma, then you have more than four hours to kill before the next one departs.

The tram leaves Soller for Puerto de Soller effectively every hour — with several extras put into the time-table around the middle of the day and at the end of the afternoon — from about 6am to 9pm. But don't worry too much if you miss the last one — it will only cost you a three-mile taxi ride or about forty-five minutes of shoe-leather.

Combined train and tram timetable issued by Ferrocarril de Soller S.A. together with second class return tickets (slightly reduced).

TRAIN TIMETABLE	
Palma departures	**Soller departures**
08.00	06.45
10.40 (tourist)	09.15
13.00	11.50
15.15	14.10
19.45	18.20
	21.00 (Sundays/ holidays only)

TRAM TIMETABLE			
Soller departures		**Port departures**	
05.55	12.30	06.20	12.30
07.00	13.00	07.30	13.00
08.00	14.00	08.25	13.25
09.00	15.00	09.30	14.30
10.00	16.00	10.30	15.30
11.00	16.30	11.30	16.30
11.30	17.00	12.00	17.00
12.00	17.55		17.30
	19.00		17.55
	20.00		18.30
	20.45		19.30
			20.20
			21.10